Challenge into Change
2013 Inspirational Essay Contest

The Women's Initiative
1101 East High Street, Suite A
Charlottesville, VA 22902
www.thewomensinitiative.org
434.872.0047

Copyright 2013 The Women's Initiative

1st Edition

ISBN 978-1-304-52978-7

All rights reserved. This book may not be reproduced, in whole or in part, in any form or by any means electronic or mechanical, including photocopying, recording or by any information storage and retrieval system now known or hereafter invented, without written permission from The Women's Initiative.

Challenge into Change

2013 Inspirational Essay Contest

Printed in USA by Lulu Press.

You may order this title through Lulu.com, Amazon.com, or by calling The Women's Initiative 434.872.0047.

DEDICATION

To all the women who share their stories with us and to all those who hold our stories.

PREFACE

The Challenge into Change Essay Contest was conceived in 2007 by former TWI Executive Director Kerry Day. Through the years, the agency and contest supporters have wrestled with whether it is appropriate for stories of this nature to compete with each other. Is it appropriate to name "winners" and award prizes?

The reason The Women's Initiative created the contest format is that we know how painful it can be to put life's truths onto paper. Finding the words to tell one's personal tale takes great courage, strength, time. The awards and prizes offered are intended to both honor this effort and also provide some incentive: a little nudge, that gentle push we sometimes need to do things we might not otherwise.

As will become clear when you read the stories that follow, they are *not* in competition with each other. Each stands on its own merits. Each is a triumph in its own right. Also note that the majority of essays (and poems) are presented as written. Some essayists elected to make minor changes prior to publication, and a small number asked us to make minor copyediting changes, if needed. We intentionally took this relaxed editing approach in order to honor each woman's words as written and to underscore that this is not a writing contest per se, but rather a forum for sharing important life stories.

We trust you will be inspired by this year's collection of essays and, perhaps, even moved to consider sharing *your* story of transformation in a future Challenge into Change Essay "Contest."

ACKNOWLEDGEMENTS

෨෬

The Women's Initiative thanks the courageous women who submitted their inspirational stories to the 2013 contest. May your stories heal, unite, and inspire all who read your words.

An essay contest cannot occur without a panel of judges who give of their time and care for each essay submitted to make the hardest decisions. Thank you:

Kerry Day, author and former Executive Director of The Women's Initiative; Pie Dumas, author and Certified Life Coach; Margaret Plews-Ogan, author and M.D. University of Virginia Health System; and Lesley Foster, experienced feature writer, copywriter, magazine editor, and writing consultant who also served as our 2013 Contest Coordinator.

Thank you Lesley for your energy, talent, and wisdom.

Much gratitude as well to our programming partners – the many local agencies that promoted this contest and often facilitated essay submittals. We value the many ways in which we work together for a strong community.

The Women's Initiative appreciates tremendously receiving a non-profit discounted rate to host this year's Final Essay Contest Celebration at the beautiful, new Jefferson School African American Heritage Center. What a lovely resource for our community.

Finally, a thousand cupfuls of thanks to our newly formed Events (non)-Committee of The Women's Initiative for their hard work to bring door prizes, publicity and financial support to this event. Thank you Joyce Holt, Kakie Brooks, Karen Boeschenstein, Kathleen Ford, Kay Forde-Mazrui, Meg Handelsman and Peggy Quayle.

TABLE OF CONTENTS

Introduction 1

Walk Slow *Beth Gager* (1st Place) 3

Momma Jean *Debbie Campbell* (2nd Place) 5

Dear God *Myra Nadine Anderson* (3rd Place) 7

A Life Altered by Choices *Keesha Johnson* (Runner Up) 11

Lose Weight *Kathleen Forde-Mazrui* (Runner Up) 13

My Friend, Laura *Jean Perry-Hayes* (Runner Up) 15

Linda *Melissa Vera Malone* (Honorable Mention) 17

The Scarlett Letters *Joyce Allan* (Honorable Mention) 19

Skydiving: A Quantum Leap Within *Renée Blue O'Connell*
(Honorable Mention) 23

The Call *Aïda Minet* 25

Today *Allison Barnes* 27

Her Transformation *Amalia* 29

Rewrite *Anne Sweazey* 31

Whole-Sum *B. Vee* 33

Change is Good *Cathy Lyons* 35

Graduating from Liberty University, A Dream Come True
Charlotte Schafer 37

Friendship *Cynthia Power* 39

What was she thinking *Deanna* 41

I'm Livin' in the Now *Diane Harrell* 43

Gene *Judith Sullivan* 45

Prescription: Yoga *Kellie L. Silcio* 47

How Did You Get Here, An Odyssey *Linda* 49

Polio: A Lifetime Challenge *Wilma T. Mangione* 51

About The Women's Initiative 53

About the Judges 55

INTRODUCTION
☙❧

When women bond together in community in such a way that "sisterhood" is created, it gives them an accepting and intimate forum to tell their stories and have them heard and validated by others. The community not only helps heal their circumstance, but encourages them to grow into their larger destiny. – Sue Monk Kidd

As Outreach Coordinator and member of the Judge's Panel for this year's essay contest, I witnessed the incredible sisterhood created "when women bond together in community" through the sharing of stories. From the launch of the contest in January, through the reading and judging of essays in late spring, to the final event celebration in June, I had a behind-the-scenes look *and* a front row seat at an event that tugged at my heart and filled it to the brim.

This book shares a selection of inspirational essays (and poems) written by women who entered the 2013 Challenge Into Change Essay Contest. Together, they explored such themes as: physical and mental abuse, mental illness, depression, disability, discrimination, violence, poverty, abandonment, job loss, starting over, teen pregnancy, raising children, faith, and finding a purpose.

During the final event, essayists read their stories aloud to a rapt crowd of family and community members whose absorbing presence paid tribute to these courageous women. Afterwards, all the essayists were honored on stage; each received a personalized certificate with poignant remarks from the contest's four judges, some of which were also read aloud to the audience.

I was struck not only by the power of the stories, but also by people's comments during the reception that followed. Many said they were hungry for more and could have listened to stories all afternoon. One essayist told me how connected she felt to those who'd shared their stories, even though she'd never met them before. "It felt like we were part of a community all rooting for one another," she said.

Even after the event, I continued to receive comments via email voicing sentiments like: "I was so touched by the thoughtful words that the judges placed on my certificate." "It meant so much to me." "I am still glowing two days later." "I felt humbled by each woman's challenges and how each recovered with dignity and strength." "Thank you for the privilege to participate."

Everyone has a story to tell. But not everyone tells it. Fewer still write the story down, read it before an audience, or allow it to be published in a collection like this. Yet personal stories of triumph over adversity are the most compelling stories of all. They are wisdom stories. Shared with others, they awaken compassion and remind us of our similarities instead of differences.

The Women's Initiative hopes that as this contest continues to evolve, more and more women will choose to share their wisdom stories because, goodness knows, the world needs all the wisdom (and compassion) it can get. The Challenge Into Change Essay Contest is a moving reminder that we must take time to tell and listen to each other's stories and that words are the true currency of human exchange.

I leave you with more wise words from author Sue Monk Kidd, which encapsulate beautifully the purpose of The Women's Initiative and this book: "I have been part of several communities of women over the years. Each of them was created simply because we wanted a place to tell our deepest stories. In every case we found that there is a way of being together that sustains us and now and then, if we are lucky, returns us to ourselves."

Lesley Foster
Contest Coordinator and Judge
2013 Challenge into Change Essay Contest
Charlottesville, VA

Walk Slow

Beth Gager

1st Place

> *The author's voice is gentle and wise. Her essay reveals a hard-earned optimism and an ability to acknowledge the life's shadows but also to swim in its inherent beauty & joy.* ❖ *The image of "feeling the ground" is wonderful.* ❖ *Excellent transformative journey! I was with you step by step.* ❖ *Your beautifully crafted essay exudes a gentle wisdom and peaceful self-awareness clearly hard-won, but enduring and certain to inspire others.*

Sometimes we have to go slow. We have to walk step by step to where we are headed. We have to feel our feet on the ground and we have to look around us and breathe. Sometimes it feels like even with all those steps we are still in the same old place. We begin to wonder if the view will ever change. And then suddenly, one day, after our feet have carried us far, we find ourselves in a new landscape. All of those steps took us somewhere we weren't sure we would ever reach. But then we look up and discover that we have actually arrived.

I am feeling like that these days. Like I have finally arrived. In a new place. A place I don't have to go back from.

There was a time when my world shattered. I tried to find myself spiritually and instead I got very, very lost. I forayed into what we call mental illness. I had a complete break from everything that kept me in the world. I went as far away from what keeps us walking on the ground as a person could go. And then came the psychiatric hospitalizations and the consequences of that. And so not only was I lost but I lost everything in my life as well…my friends, my job, my children, my home.

The result was that for a long time after that I had to walk slow. For many years I got very heavy physically and mentally and spiritually. I slowly rebuilt my life step by step. I got back what I had lost. But I wanted more. I wanted not only my life back but also my most essential self back. I didn't want to be heavy any more. I wanted to walk with joy in my step again. I wanted to remember what it felt like to have a connection with my spirit and with the earth and with the people around me. So I began walking differently. I began letting myself feel my heart again.

I literally began by walking. I walked in my neighborhood. I noticed the trees and the sky and I paid attention to how my body felt. I started doing yoga. I began to eat better. And I walked differently inside myself as well. I slowly, slowly began reconnecting to my spirituality. I began to meditate and pray. Every time I hit a place that was a scary reminder of where I had been I took a new step forward away from fear and toward beauty and love.

And now I find myself in a new place. A place where I remember but also where I can rest. I can walk when I want to. And I do want to. But I can also sit down under an old tree and enjoy what is all around me. I can be present in a quiet way inside myself. And that was worth the long, hard walk.

Momma Jean
Debbie Campbell

2nd Place

> *A beautifully rendered portrait of "faith, dignity and grace." I can see "Momma Jean" sitting in your sewing room, and am inspired by your powerful ability to find hope in everything and express gratitude with every breath.* ❖ *What a moving tribute to your mother and the life-long lessons she taught by her own example.* ❖ *Momma Jean is a mythical symbol for bravery, love and faith captured by the women of your family.* ❖ *Your story draws the reader immediately into the soft, warm, "graceful" environment your mother created despite difficult circumstances.*

Momma Jean is old and worn now. She is wearing a torn dress with a thread bare face, but her embroidered blue eyes look as happy as the childhood I remember. Now, sitting in my sewing room, she is a reminder that it is possible to transform poverty to beauty and overcome challenges with faith, dignity and grace.

I must have been four years old when my mother made her on the old sewing machine that sat in our kitchen. I watched as she tore open an ancient pillow and filled Momma Jean with feathers. She braided yellow yarn for hair, cut her favorite red dress into one for the doll and finished it with a bright, cheerful smile. This doll became my best friend. Every night I snuggled my face securely to hers and had no idea of the poverty we lived in.

It wasn't until I was an adult that I became aware that catastrophic illnesses left my young parents in poverty. To keep creditors from our door my father worked multiple jobs. My mother stayed at home with us children and learned to change her response to their many struggles from an overwhelming depression into creative productivity. She did everything she could imagine to transform our crude house into a cozy home.

Sitting up late at night, she smocked dresses and sewed pretty aprons for me. I had a beautiful wardrobe made with such skill that they rivaled any Polly Flinder dress my school friends wore. Each piece cut from a second hand garment. I remember one hot summer my mother collected wool coats, jackets and slacks that were moth eaten, stained and discarded, unfit for wear. For weeks she cut, twisted, turned and tugged at them until a beautiful braided rug emerged. Her loving efforts made three rugs that warmed our home for the next fifteen years.

My parents worked hard and eventually paid off their medical bills. We moved from a small apartment into a home they built with their own hands. Even then, frugality was woven into their marriage and into our home. Mom taught us to be grateful for even the small things.

My mother is my role model. I so admire her ability to remain strong and faithful in the face of so many adversities. So when I was married at twenty, I, like her, lived in poverty. I drew from her example to transform the raw elements that surrounded me to create a cozy home for my children to grow in. Over the years I have learned to sew and have built my own fashion business from scratch.

I want to pass on the legacy that belongs to the women in my family. We may face many hardships in this life, but we can change the way we view our circumstances and find true prosperity through resourcefulness, hard work and faithfulness.

Dear God
Myra Nadine Anderson

3rd Place

> *Your moving and eloquent poem demonstrates the remarkable transformative power of words in your life and how they helped you heal from and transcend unthinkable events.* ❖ *The author's repetition of the phrase "I need these words" is potent, as is her symbolic and powerful representation of wounds that must be healed.* ❖ *Your voice resonates with sincerity as you speak your prayerful words to God.*

Dear God,

There is a hole deep in my heart

It comes for being wounded when I was younger

The perpetrators stole my youth and my innocence

They stole it like thieves in the night

I imagine now I must find a way to heal this hole

This gaping wound

That lets my trust seep through

That lets my faith seep through

That lets my sanity seep through

I imagine now I must find words to symbolize the tiny sutures needed to mend my broken heart

For years now I have been wounded

Wounded by the atrocity of being left in the wilderness for the wild to prey upon

Wounded by my endless years of struggle

I do not wish to decorate this experience with eloquent words or keen insight.

I need these words

I need these words to protect me when no one else did

I need these words because I was made to feel dirty and ashamed

I need these words so that I can stop eating away the guilt and shame

I need these words to combat the depression, sorrow, loneliness, and pain

Words mean everything to me

These words are meant to create freedom for those still in mental bondage

Liberate the souls of the oppressed, and transform the scared victim into a phenomenal survivor

I declare with these words that God you love me, you love us all, and that I am worthy

Whether I conquer this depression or not

Whether I marry and have kids or not

Whether I lose weight or not

Even if my friends betray me and my family forsakes me

I'm still worthy

I was worthy before the molestations, rape, and abuse

& I'm worthy now

I declare that I have overcome many obstacles and accomplished a great deal

But God I know you have so much more in store for me,

So, I will continue writing these words FIRST, for self-reflection

SECOND, for discovery of hole that needs mending

And THIRD, to share with my sisters who have fallen victim to the wolves in the night

God, you can heal us all and these are healing words

All sorrows can be
borne if we put them in
a story or tell a story
about them.

- Isak Dinesen

A Life Altered by Choices
Keesha Johnson

Runner Up

> *Your heart-rending story of persevering against the odds in your lifelong dream to be educated and attend college is sure to be a beacon to others.* ❖ *A true story of overcoming all odds and creating a path, lined with good choices, for a successful and promise-filled future.* ❖ *A story of great perseverance.* ❖ *Your story is hopeful and brave.*

I've always wanted to go to college. In life, you always hear people say you have a choice. However, there were times in my life in which I did not have choices. I have a son who is a product of statutory rape. No choice there. Growing up as a teenager, my friends were drug dealers, bank robbers, street enforcers, or people who took the law into their own hands. I became a drug dealer, too.

My mother and mainly, my stepfather never trusted or forgave me for having a baby at fourteen-years of age. One argument too many ended up with me being homeless. I was hurt and broken. My son ended up staying with his paternal grandmother because I couldn't support him.

Prospect Avenue, located on the south side of Charlottesville, Virginia, was seen as the slums, as it was across the railroad tracks and was a housing project. On Prospect, one could find drug dealers, and of course, crack heads. There were adults and children who had no rules or regulations. Any and everything goes.

Before having my son, and when I was on the basketball team, I would always practice my dribbling up and down the block, pass the drug deals, gangsters and the miss-guided. My dribbling skills wouldn't let them steal my ball. It was a good game of cat and mouse.

Looking in my past life, I have been present when people were shot and, unfortunately, I saw a baby killed by a stray a bullet. Because of lifestyle choices, I've been stabbed, and beaten by a gang of men that I did not know. Circumstances caused me to turn on those who attacked, causing me to behave like an abuser.

I have had my apartment riddled with bullets, scared for my life. During this incident, my elderly neighbor fell breaking her hip. She became a nursing home resident.

Stuck in the street life, I have now come out of the fog of confusion, and parental neglect and realize that what happened in the past is just that, the past. During those times I felt I had no choices. Decisions were made for me because of my environment, my immaturity because of my neglected.

My dream was always to be educated.

I left a situation in Miami, Fla., in December 2012, without a job, but had a desire to learn, and to mend my family situation, and to be successful.

Today, I am a student in the GED program, attending the Adult Learning Center, in Charlottesville, VA. Since January 2013, I have taken four of the GED tests, and have passed them. Therefore, I will take my fifth test, which is math, and I expect to pass it too. After successfully completing my GED, I will begin my dream of attending college in Miami. There are no limits. Yes, we all have choices. I will choose my future, and I chose to have a successful future.

Lose Weight
Kathleen Forde-Mazrui

Runner Up

This moving essay shows that by caring for our bodies, we also care for our souls. ❖ *The warmth and humor with which you told your story speaks volumes about your radiant inner appearance as well.* ❖ *Wow! Inspiring story, love your food descriptions, commitment and dedication.* ❖ *The lifelong weight challenge you faced and overcame is truly inspiring.*

"Lose weight," said a young man I did not know as he passed my near 200 pound 20 year old body. I did not take his kind advice until I was closer to 400 pounds and 40 years of age.

In sixth grade my parents allowed my school counselor to take me to Weight Watcher's. There were very few overweight children in my school. I was a special case. I did lose weight and Weight Watcher's was always the program I returned to when I was moved to try to stem my ever increasing girth.

Is there anything more delicious and comforting than McDonald's cheeseburgers and fries? And because it would be gluttonous to eat more than two cheeseburgers and one large order of fries, what more delicious and comforting way to keep eating than with a bag of barbeque Chex Mix sprinkled over a big bowl of popcorn.

At 40 years of age and 360 pounds "the pain of staying the same must have become worse than the pain of changing" because I joined Weight Watcher's once again and over the next two years lost over 200 pounds. I've maintained a healthy weight since.

What was different this time?

The Weight Watcher's program had evolved. The dieter had complete freedom to choose what foods to eat within a recommended caloric limit. I planned and ate delicious food. If one chose high fiber, low calorie foods, more food could be consumed. I learned that beans (so many lovely kinds) and egg whites and tofu and fish are the lowest calorie choices for protein. I substituted a bed of lettuce for rice or pasta – yes, a lentil curry over lettuce instead of rice, marinara sauce with a ground beef substitute and all the usual vegetables over lettuce instead of pasta. I read labels and found the lowest calorie, highest fiber tortilla (LaTortilla Factory), delicious Triple Succotash (Margaret Holmes) and the lowest calorie waffle on the market (Van's Light). If you find a lower one let me know!

The first week I concentrated only on the diet aspect of weight loss, I did no exercise. Then I slowly added exercise. The first day of the second week I could barely walk the length of my city block, arriving home to collapse in a pool of sweat on the couch, vowing to do nothing more than lay there for the rest of the day. In the beginning I exercised five out of seven days, then six. After a time I did not want to let a day go by without walking which I had increased to two miles. After losing the weight I rediscovered my childhood love of riding a bicycle, which is now my main exercise.

Finally, in the beginning, at night, when there was no more food to eat, I cried. Tears have no calories. Each morning I woke up happy that I had not overeaten. I am not crying anymore because nothing tastes as good as healthy feels.

My Friend, Laura

Jean Perry-Hayes

Runner Up

Laura deserves a standing ovation for surviving and thriving amidst such hardship. Thank you for caring for her and sharing her story. ❖ *I am astonished and moved by how Laura continued to press forward in her life despite such unrelenting adversity.* ❖ *The author writes with a potent blend of honesty, conviction and optimism.* ❖ *An inspiring story of courage told with great admiration.*

When Laura was an infant she was left in the care of her grandmother, Columba, when her parents separated. Laura grew to be close to her grandmother and through her teen years Laura spent much of her life at hospitals, due to her grandmother's illnesses. Soon she had to learn the matters related to growing crops to assure that the house have enough income to be sustained. Laura's mother never visited and her father saw her once a year.

When Laura was 21, her grandmother died, leaving her alone. To avoid fighting with her family she gave up her inheritance and lived with friends. She began working in a factory. At 26 she started written communication with a man that lived in the United States. Through their interactions, the relationship grew and he sent for her. Soon after coming to the U.S., Laura became pregnant. She wanted to keep her baby, but the father did not. He began to aggressively her. When her daughter was born, the father wanted to keep the baby but not Laura. He continued to mistreat and abuse her; he even put a gun to her head trying to take away her daughter. Laura, fearing for their safety, ran to Mexico, without knowing that the persecution she endured would continue over there even by armed guards that he paid off.

When her daughter was three, Laura and her daughter came back to U.S. Although her child is an American citizen, her documents were stolen and she had to cross the border undocumented. Laura became depressed and her daughter began presenting behavioral problems. They rented one bedroom in a dark mobile home; there was domestic violence between the couple renting the other bedroom. Laura and her daughter spent much time inside the only safe place in the home, their room. Making matters worse, the father of Laura's daughter began to threaten the family again. This time because of her great fear of this man and a need for help Laura and her daughter ran, to the SHE shelter. At the Shelter, Laura found Dilcia Colindres who was always a great support to her. Laura had counselors who treated her depression. She found a job and an apartment to rent with a friend. After a month she was left with the full responsibility of the new place. With motivation and determination Laura was able to save money, buy a car and learn to drive.

Now, Laura is a happier woman, She has been able to maintain the same bright apartment for over 4 years, works independently, and is totally involved in her daughter's life; who is a bright student, a cheerleader for her school, part of the basketball team and attending Church every week. Laura is a health promoter and is a leading hand. She helps other families learn about community resources, amongst many other things and gives volunteer hours to various organizations. Although she cannot drive currently, nothing will stop her now. She is moving forward!

Linda
Melissa Vera Malone

Honorable Mention

> *Your moving tribute to your mother is a powerful reminder that we must never let circumstances dictate the outcome and possibilities for our lives.* ❖ *An inspiring essay honoring a woman whose life story epitomizes courage, perseverance and transformation.* ❖ *This essay is filled with love and gratitude.* ❖ *A true testimony to your love and pride for your mother.*

In 1979 my mother's dream of becoming a doctor ended. She was told by Admissions that a "young mother of two would not be able to emotionally and/or physically complete medical school." A year later she ended an unhappy marriage and set out to change her life. She took a secretarial position at a small law firm, and fought for the custody of her children.

I do not know if it was her own legal battles, seeing the battles of others, or simply her need of feeling well prepared in her job that led her to reading the law. My mother was an avid reader, and she poured her passion into texts and journals. She never took any courses throughout her studies; instead she registered for the Bar Exam to see what she was up against. "Just a little practice" she told me on our drive to Roanoke for her first attempt. My mother took the Bar Exam three times, and in 1986 we travelled to Richmond to watch my mother, my brilliant mother, who never went to law school, get sworn into the Virginia State Bar Association. She wore a red silk blouse, setting her apart from the sea of black and gray suits. At eleven years old, I knew to be proud.

For the next two decades my mother used the power of her law degree to help other single parents, children, and families with their legal battles. She was giving back.

In less than a decade my mother drastically changed her life. She turned her disappointment into success by not letting the world dictate her path. She chose a new one. My mother's journey constantly reminds me to allow for change, and that disappointment may offer new opportunities. Her life reminds me that the greatest rewards come from hard work, self-discipline, and an open mind.

I did not learn of my mother's rejection from medical school until her passing in 2003. It was then that we also learned that my brother and I were the cause for her rejection. She never conveyed her disappointment, or showed any resentment towards us. She respected us, and we therefore respected and adored her. She was a powerful role model. An individual.

In preparation of my mother's eulogy I jotted down a list of words describing her life's journey. Each word: a reminder of a moment, an accomplishment, a passion, an unspoken promise, a love, or an ideal of who she was. Each word from the list would reveal a story of change and strength of character. Those words, an incomplete list, feel the same today as they did a decade ago, and for me still bring the same conclusion. She was such a brilliant lady.

The Scarlet Letters
Joyce Allan

Honorable Mention

Raw, painful and inspiring, this essay speaks of a woman with the power to overcome her past, release injustice, and build a better future. ❖ Sandra's story is testament to the strength of the human spirit. Her character and integrity shine throughout this piece offering hope to others finding their way through adversity. ❖ A poignant story that shows how, with perseverance and courage, things can change and the evil of the past does not have to dictate the future.

Sandra was raised in poverty and violence.

At age 16 she began a relationship with an emotionally and physically abusive man and considered this a "normal" marriage. She gave birth to her first child, a premature baby girl with severe physical disabilities. Sandra's life could never be normal now.

She was mother to a child who would need ceaseless medical care, special education, multiple surgeries, and constant emotional support. Sandra learned her way through the medical, educational and social service systems. Her daughter's care was her mission in life.

A new infant, a disabled toddler, bankruptcy and domestic violence locked her into a life of responsibility, exhaustion, and fear. Sandra was living in "difficult circumstances." And there was no change.

Eight years later Sandra escaped. She utilized the women's shelter and DSS (Department of Social Services), moved temporarily into her parents' small home. She was placed under CPS (Child Protective Services) supervision, enrolled her children in new schools, and worked full time.

Sandra's life was now "differently difficult." She was not being beaten and berated, but she had no place to live. For others in this situation, there might be some "safety net" for a responsible, working mother with two children. Sandra's real challenge was just beginning. She was a newly convicted Sex Offender.

You see, the incident that motivated Sandra to escape was that her husband brought his teen-age girlfriend into their home. At gun point he forced Sandra, their two daughters, and the teenager to play "strip poker." Sandra had taken his violence, but this new humiliation of her daughters crossed the line – her determination to keep them safe.

In the ugly aftermath of reporting the strip poker to Social Services, Sandra herself was charged as a Sex Offender for "exposing her genitals" to her children. Absurd as this may seem, she was convicted and added to the Virginia State Sex Offender Registry.

By law, she'd committed a felony. Rape, child sexual abuse, having consensual relations with a 17- year old, or urinating in public can be equal felonies. There is no pardon, no appeal. Registry as a Sex Offender is for life.

Since 2004 Sandra has worn the Scarlet Letters S.O. "Sex Offender." Therefore, public and non-profit agencies routinely deny her services. Pursuit of housing, jobs, education, and friends always requires disclosure. Disclosure is often followed by rejection, shaming, and shunning.

Trapped by injustice, Sandra has never wavered from her commitment to raise her daughters. She knows that escaping her marriage was brave, that being a poor, single mother is hard, that life is not fair. She knows that she is strong and intelligent.

And, she knows that she is not a Sex Offender.

Sandra has obtained a divorce, found a new job, earned credits at PVCC community college and paid her bills. Her daughters have finished high school. A new phase of her life is beginning.

Though she can never be free of the stigma her Sex Offender label brings, Sandra's determination, responsibility, dignity and gratitude for the blessings in her life continue to inspire me.

She is a SHE Ro! She is not an S.O.

"There is no agony like bearing an untold story inside of you."

-Maya Angelou

Skydiving: A Quantum Leap Within
Renée Blue O'Connell

Honorable Mention

> *The symbolic representation of finding flight – and regaining an ability to hear life's music – is beautiful and profound.* ❖ *Beautifully orchestrated and crafted. Heartfelt!* ❖ *A powerful reminder that it is never too late to follow your dreams.* ❖ *A beautiful story of courage, stepping into opportunity, and using one's gifts to make the world a better place.*

My dream of becoming a professional musician ignited as a teenager when I began playing the guitar. I became very serious about it and studied classical guitar in Chicago.

Twenty-eight years ago I encountered my first obstacle when another music student invited me to hear a new piece he composed. I waited for what seemed like a long time. Finally, I asked, "When are you going to play me your new piece?"

He said, "I just did—didn't you hear it?"

I did not.

That was how I learned I had a profound hearing loss. I was 25 years old.

I was fitted for a hearing aid, but over the years my hearing worsened. Oddly enough, I never felt it interfered with my music. It did, however, create obstacles in communicating with others. I could play my guitar in a coffee house, yet I couldn't hear well enough over the phone to book performances. I just didn't have the confidence in my hearing ability to represent myself. How could I convince others that I am a good musician even though I am profoundly deaf? Who would hire such a person?

So, I played it safe and took a job as an office assistant. There I stayed for 14 years, alone in a windowless office in front of a computer. Many days I felt discouraged. I wanted to make a difference. I wanted my life to mean more than a job that did not inspire me.

Three years ago, I had the life changing experience of undergoing cochlear implant surgery.

I can still remember that cold January morning very well. I had never been hospitalized and what could have been a frightening ordeal turned out to be one of the most touching experiences of my life. My surgeon was like a friend to me. When he came in the room, I reached out to him and asked, "Are you ready for me?" He held my hand and asked "Are *you* ready for me?" I nodded. Then he said, "I'm proud of you. " That's the last thing I remember before the *anesthesia* took effect.

Now, here I am with the best hearing I have ever had. Because of this procedure, I am now working as a professional musician. I am a certified music practitioner and I play for patients, seniors and disabled young adults. Each day I do the work I feel I am meant to be doing in the world. Dreams do come true.

For my 50th birthday, I wanted to go skydiving to ring in the next phase of my life. Instead, I got a cochlear implant. Little did I know how much this journey to hear again would be much like skydiving. I took a risk and found my wings to fly above the obstacles that once held me back. Because of this, I found new heights I never knew were there.

The Call
Aïda Minet

> *A true story of one who overcomes the depths of depression by reaching out to others, and ultimately, reconnecting with the forever present beauty of her spirit.* ❖ *Your story is a poignant example of how others' support can help us find our way, but only if we choose to reach out and grab the outstretched hand. The strength and courage you showed in reaching past your fear is sure to offer hope and encouragement to others struggling to find their way.* ❖ *Your essay captures your gratitude for Bill & Mrs. Ramos – I "feel" your movement and triumph through your words!* ❖ *The author tells a compelling story of how, with encouragement from friends, we CAN DO!*

In the abyss of my sadness, in the precise moment that everything moves in slow motion and you see everything stops and is frozen. Everything you fought and worked to achieve falls through your hands, and your mind is just empty. In that moment I was ready to separate from this world. In that precise moment I received the most needed phone call. It was a phone call that broke my fall. I heard words of encouragement, words my own parents never said to me. I was given an opportunity to start over. The opportunity was there in front of me offering its hand for me to hold it on tightly and pull out of darkness.

It was my best friend Bill calling to give me moral support and an opportunity to start over by offering refuge in his home and helping me to find myself. As you can expect from a civil engineer, he thought he could fix me. He wanted me to improve my life. He challenged me to do everything on my part to help myself. The days were passing by and he did not observe any improvement in me, so he decided to be more rigid with me. "Can you deal with this?" He looked me in the eyes and said that he didn't want to participate in my depression cycle, and with a loud voice he said: "Can you or can't you?"

A big challenge was ahead of me. Time passed by and little by little I started gaining strength to meet that challenge. That is when I decided to leave the house to find help. I had the good fortune to find The Women's Initiative. They helped my path. I must say thank you to Mrs. Ramos for her understanding and motivation for this new path that my life has taken. My life journey has not been easy. However I fight and achieve the objectives that I set up for myself. In this point in time I am setting up my own business. It is something small, and through my work I can express my gratitude to Bill and Mrs. Ramos. The process has been slow, but I am stronger than ever. A testament to my character. I was able to break free from the stuck pattern of my life.

Today I run *Cuba 52* at the Charlottesville City Market serving the foods of my native Cuba. It was always a dream of mine to open a restaurant, and the City Market is an expression of that dream. I couldn't have done what I did without the help of Mrs. Ramos and Bill.

Today I say: "I could and I can!" The challenge is done. Mission accomplished. I am laughing, and playing—the way I am . . . proudly Cubana. Challenges are difficult, but not impossible. At my 60 years of age I have been able to do it. I hope my story brings comfort to any person that is discouraged. I hope that the person can find an opportunity like the one I found and can take advantage of it.

Now I can laugh and I am thankful for my life. ¡Que viva siempre mi querida Cuba!

Today
Allison Barnes

> *Faith reigns supreme in this moving essay about loss and love.* ❖ *Your rhyme and phrasing are rhythmically pleasing; in tune with a forgiving, accepting heart.* ❖ *The reader can feel the love you have for your nephew and that God has for you.* ❖ *Thank you for sharing your story of faith that sustained and continues to sustain you in the face of loss of one you held so dear.*

Today is a good day, they say

Even if you have a bad day

Because there is a man above

that shows his love

And he loves us all

whether big or small

Because from the lessons I have learned only makes me want to yearn

Yearn to let each person know

that life isn't promised as we all know

Today you have a chance to let someone you know I love you so

Please smile for for we are just here for a little while

Each day we live, we must give

Gods love as we knows and tell the devil no

For 6 months ago in September I endured the worst day I ever had

So each day I live I can be oh so glad

Glad enough to know that even though I am grieving the loss of my nephew

God sees me, and letting me know that my nephew, and God still loves me so

He comes to me in my dreams, and sometimes letting me know things are not as hard as they seam

For I today have the treasure to know that Michael, God, and I love you so.

Her Transformation
Amalia

> *Genuine and heartfelt, this essay reveals the story of a woman who has overcome an abusive past and miraculously retained her belief in the precious quality of "the innermost space of the heart."* ❖ *Your story demonstrates not only your profound inner strength to heal from violence, but is also a moving example of how to live from the heart and light the way for others.* ❖ *A loving, positive tribute to your "favoritest" friend. Your expressive support for "her" is uplifting and enriching.*

My dearest sweet friend,

I'm so very proud and blessed to have you in my life. You have overcome more than you may ever truly know. The love and wisdom that you are able to share because of you horrific experience is a great blessing that touches every person you encounter.

I cannot imagine the heartache pain and strife your extremely violent abusive marriage caused you. I just know the beautiful transformation that has emerged into who you are now and becoming.

Being stripped of all dignity, respect and self-worth was your rock bottom. Not being able to even see the tunnel, let alone the light at the end of the tunnel must have been very bleak and lonely.

I pray you can feel deep in your heart you are truly loved by many and deserve so much better than to be treated in such a debilitatingly heinous way.

Your story exudes hope in every aspect.

I remember what you thought when he'd called you his lil solider. Your heart was screaming, "Yeah, but he is fighting for the wrong side!" You are an honorable warrior fighting on the side of righteousness with strengthened testimonies on your side. I'm so blessed to be a witness of Christ's transformation within your heart as well as your life and the lives you've been able to be such a positive influence to.

You're truly an amazing person who carries the greatest spirit inside your heart. Words do no justice for the wonderful person you are and forever will be.

I admire how you love like you've never been hurt. Sing like nobody is listening and dance as if no one is watching!

The non-judgmental way you support others is inspiring to me. How you find ways to care for those who feel unloved. Your natural innate ability to see through the disheveled, dysfunctional outer layer of a person and grasp the inner most spaces of their heart. Leaves a lasting hopeful impression on their souls!

The life you're now choosing to live is not dictated by your past. It's a part of you giving you this over whelming ability of survival. The chains of guilt and shame placed on you by the abuse are dissolving away freeing you from the heavy burdens of inequity. I feel like the grace of God has saved you. Now He is able to use you as a beacon for others to emerge into the light and away from the darkness that was threatening to consume you.

You have most definitely come the long way, down the roughest road traveled. But you are no longer fighting the good fight alone. You have many on your side cheering and encouraging you on. You are one of my "favoritest" people in this whole entire world.

Your positive influence of strength enduring through the tough times is an immeasurable wonderful influence to us All!

So very much Love and Aloha, Your #1 Fan,

~*~Me~*~

P.S. Rock on with your bad self!

Rewrite

Anne Sweazey

> *Poetically rendered, this essay sheds light on the way in which painful memories do not have to define the people we become. "We can stretch our limbs, emerge and find ... an unseen truth." Lovely rewrite, without negating the past.* ❖ *You offer a hopeful and compelling message that no matter how painful our past it is possible to emerge from "a tight, dark place" and find "unseen possibility."* ❖ *You show great insight into how, with a different lens on our experience, we can see the good, the opportunity, the strength in ourselves and others.* ❖ *Elegantly bearing witness to your retelling, re-examination and recreating the heart-full truth of possibility.*

"I've been working on my rewrite, that's right. I'm gonna change the ending. Gonna throw away my title. And toss it in the trash."
-Paul Simon

This is the story of my Rewrite. My Rewrite was my way of redefining my life experiences. The true intention was to write my future the way I wanted to see it. What I wrote however, started from my first day on earth and ended present day. In an unexpected way, that was enough.

My Rewrite was simple and changed the lens I used to view the past. For example, a lot of us had extraordinarily tough childhoods for one or many reasons. I wasn't protected or well cared for. True. What is also true is that I was loved. That's where I began. "Once upon a time there was a little girl born to a Mommy, Daddy and two brothers who loved her very much."

It's important to know I wasn't turning rose-colored glasses on the past. Bad stuff happened and had to be recognized. This was pulling the flowers from the weeds.

As I worked on my Rewrite, reading through what I had written, I was amazed how true it felt…because it was. I consolidated years of my life, the brighter parts. In two and a half pages I had rewritten my entire life, birth to 37. Still today, reading my Rewrite is relief from a heavy story I have carried for years.

The last six years of my life were the most painful to reexamine. Mental illness and long stored memories of abuse crept into my world (and my new marriage) and life turned in a way I never could have imagined. What looked like the hard won opportunity for love and safety became the most confusing and terrifying of all I'd been through. Those shame and regret-filled years were always in my rear view mirror. To move forward with my Rewrite, and through those memories, I retold the magic of meeting my husband, the beauty of our wedding and the endurance we displayed. The section that followed, I'll share.

"Hard times fell again, prince and princess, husband and wife, turned man and woman. Uncomfortably human and in it together. The sun rose slowly. The light returned almost imperceptibly. Sometimes she saw the light and sometimes it was him but rarely did they see it together. Sad, not to have a shared sense of warmth, but perhaps just as well that each held the light for the other. The flame flickered low at times but never, ever went out."

That was my challenge.

This is my change.

"As the sun rose high, husband and wife rubbed their eyes and stretched their limbs emerging from a tight, dark place. The trees were full, the leaves were green and there, once again, was possibility."

That is the point of my story…the sun can rise high, we can stretch our limbs, emerge and find an unseen possibility and in particular, an unseen truth.

Whole-Sum

(and other interesting bits you didn't know)
B. Vee

> *Your story conveys that your healing began with your choices: courage, compassion, gratitude, and a decision to heal. What gifts you give to the world. You call everyone "Sunshine," but it is clear you are the "Sunshine" in this story.* ❖ *Your essay captures the power of movement, determined mission of change, and resolve that is palpable.* ❖ *"Whole-sum" is full of inspiring bits and pieces, which together takes the author forward.* ❖ *A reminder that the heartache, brutal reality and glowing transformation of others' life stories can be instruments for change...not just for one, but for many.*

She calls everyone Sunshine. I guess it's her way of acknowledging the goodness hidden in everyone. She remembers the all-too-important and oft-forgotten Golden Rule. She believes that *every human being makes a choice to be a good person*. She holds that truth close to her as she faces her own challenges—and that's why I want you to meet her.

Though she's been through a lot, she knows someone, somewhere, RIGHT NOW shares her struggle. Her survival fuels her immense gratitude.

It's a very rare occasion when She will share her story. And I mean *the whole tale—not* the G-rated Reader's Digest condensed edition. When you are "chosen" for the telling, be aware. It's an ugly story. It will HURT to hear it . . .

It starts out like ghost story as She revisits the earliest hurts . . . then the graphic details, dirty language & nightmares flay you as She RELIVES each and every memory . . .

There's even an eerie soundtrack. *Her little-girl voice cracks and s-stutters in distress, then rage strips it to low growl* . . . Then *SNAP—it's* gone. *The waterworks evaporate, a heavy door booms shut . . . and unsteady feet make their way back up the mental staircase . . .*

It's not a fun ride for HER—because She takes *you* there.

Courage isn't given. It's bought at an immeasurable price: PAIN.

You have to fight **fiercely** for something you value. Help comes to those that are willing to heal themselves. This transforms all the pain into a new entity: Compassion. Armed with Compassion & Courage like a bow & arrow, you can aim for a much bigger target. With practice, a remarkable thing happens: YOU CHANGE.

Her life has been defined by change. Being the first female in her family to be born in the States, she adopted a new language & culture. She was the first in her family to attend college. She's had a variety of public service opportunities—one of which was unexpectedly serving the Dalai Lama. This particular experience paved her spiritual walk in Eastern practices, which later prompted her conversion to Western Christianity.

With no formal training, she writes music to share messages of encouragement with the world. In turn, her relationships with her beloved husband, her "mostly American" family & loyal friends continue to edify and nurture her . . .

She is forever changing.

She no longer struggles to fill the void that circumstance created, nor is She a shattered mess resulting from a series of "unfortunate mishaps." She is a *whole-sum* being because She is now multi-faceted & completely solid. Her resolve maintains my motivation.

Her transformation of poison to medicine in her life helps me to be joyful each day, no matter what's ahead. I face it happily. I'm grateful for the strength She's instilled in me—and the next time I'm brushing my teeth in the mirror, *I will not hesitate to thank her myself.*

Change is Good
Cathy Lyons

> *Your story is a true testament to the power and depth of the spirit to reinvent yourself, taking up roots and all, replanting in more fertile ground. Thank you for sharing your courage.* ❖ *What a story of creativity in the face of difficulty! Like a cat you land on your feet and explore your new world, knowing you can make something great out of it!* ❖ *Despite the hardship this author has endured, her essay rings with optimism and a playful, creative approach to life. Bravissimo! I love the line: "The worst that can happen is I grow my own food!"* ❖ *Yours is an inspiring story of unflagging optimism and courage providing a blueprint for how to rise above life's challenges and always find "the good in anything bad."*

I have had many ups and downs in my life, but have always managed to stay afloat through constant learning, curiosity, courage to try new things, creative thinking, tenacity, friends and family, and faith that it will all work out.

My most recent problem was losing my job through budget cuts in late 2008. At the time, I wasn't too worried since I had lots of experience and was a certified project management professional. But, after several interviews and not getting offers, (something that had never happened before) I realized that I was not only a victim of the recession, but of age. I was 60 at the time.

After 18 months of unemployment with unemployment compensation gone, savings dwindling, uncontrollable costs rising, I had to do something different and live where it was cheaper. I am very healthy and strong and was not ready nor could afford to retire, so started researching an area of endeavor that I loved from past experience. I started collecting Social Security at the age of 62, fixed up my condo for sale (which took 16 months to sell) and purchased property in Madison County to start an organic farm.

I moved from Fairfax County in June 2012 at the age of 63, purchased a tractor and needed equipment with the equity in the condo sale, started preparing land and planted a few things. Now, with the soil tests done last year and proper amendments applied, I am growing spring crops in a 5,500 sq. ft. area, with another 10,000 sq. ft. ready for summer crops. I have signed up as a producer in the Madison County Farmers Market, and will be able to start supplementing my social security benefits. I will expand the operations next year and hire some help. I plan to have about 2 acres intensively and organically farmed to build up a business that I can just manage when I am unable to perform the physical labor.

I am considering organic certification and will eventually expand my marketing to other locations and areas, such as Customer Supported Agriculture share membership, taking on a business partner, selling to restaurants and schools.

By the way, shortly after I moved here, I was welcomed by many neighbors and discovered that I own a portion of what was once a family farm. The descendants live all around me, helping and caring for each other. This inspired me to name the farm: Good Roots.

I have followed many paths in my life, all of which I learned from and enjoyed most of the time. I have always found the good in anything bad and have kept a positive attitude. My current path is the most satisfying so far, utilizing all the things that I have learned from the others. Some people have tactfully hinted that I am too old to do this. I answer: "The worst thing that can happen is I grow my own food!"

Graduating from Liberty University, A Dream Come True

Charlotte Schafer

> *What a moving story of perseverance and faith in the face of life's trials. A touching affirmation of how we must never give up on our dreams.* ❖ *A moving story of a mother & daughter who hold fast to their academic and lifelong dreams and support one another through the winds of turmoil and adversity.* ❖ *Thank you for sharing your transformed spirit with the world and for turning your messages from God into action steps.* ❖ *The writer displays courage, openness and deep gratitude in this essay.*

In 1982 I began a journey, that has begun a lifelong learning process, when I received my GED, I was then 30 years old, with two little school aged children, whom I homeschooled for six years thereafter.

Then in 1992 I became a born again believer. I had an experience with God and fell under his convicting power. After that experience, I wasn't sure what God wanted to do with my life, so I asked Him, and it seemed to me that he was saying, "Charlotte, the world is your apple, go out and find what you are good at, and do it." So that is what I did. I enrolled at a Junior college, and began taking a few classes after work. It was hard and I was tired a great deal of the time. Then the bottom fell out of my world.

My daughter now in her early 20's began showing signs of colitis, and this turned into what they would finally term crones colitis. While I was trying to work and to go college she became a very sick girl very fast, finally losing from her 5'7" frame down to a mere 95 pounds. However, after two surgeries she recovered, and graduated from her four year college, the same year I graduated from the Junior college with my Associates Degree. I was proud of both of us.

I had always wanted to go to Liberty University, but I had to accept that this was only a pipe dream. Then in 2008, we moved from Tennessee to Virginia in what I can only call a true act of God. My daughter broke off a relationship with a guy and decided to get away, not looking to date for a very long time she just wanted to visit a friend of the family, who just happened to live at Lake Monticello, Virginia.

That week my daughter met the man of her dreams while she was there. They were both ready to settle down with the right person and within six weeks their fate was sealed. He proposed on his knees in Gatlinburg, TN, and we were all thrilled. They were so in love and it was so beautiful to see.

We sold the only house we'd ever had, and moved into a basement apartment for nine long months while our 1354 square foot sweet country cottage was being built for us at Lake Monticello, Virginia. They were married in 2002, and have blessed us with two beautiful grandkids. My daughter is a beautiful accomplished amazing mom.

While finishing up my BS at Liberty University online I found myself being ministered to in nearly every course. I was healing from a life of turmoil. Now this spring, I will take part in the commencement of Liberty University and walk across the stage with hundreds of other students, in front of my grandchildren and children. Indeed this is a dream come true.

Friendship
Cynthia Power

> *A beautiful story of friendship and how your patience and willingness to lovingly confront Mary helped forge a lasting relationship.* ❖ *A moving essay about trust, honesty, and the bonds of friendship.* ❖ *Reading this essay I was immediately drawn into the community of this relationship.* ❖ *Your determination speaks volumes about how you value friendship.*

"Hello, Cynthia. It's Mary. I'm sorry but I can't go to the circus this evening. I don't feel well."

My stomach knotted. "But Mary," I said, "you told me yesterday that you wanted to go. I've paid for tickets and I can't get my money back."

"I know. I'm really sorry. I have a headache."

"Okay," I replied, and hung up, fists clenched.

The next day she left a message on my voice mail. "Hi, Cynthia. I'm so sorry. I had a previous commitment. I know I should have told you. I am sorry."

I met Mary two and a half years earlier at Radford University at a Leadership Academy which trained people with mental illness to organize and advocate for themselves. I was a trainer and Mary a trainee, signifying only that we were at different places in our recovery. Realizing that we both lived in Charlottesville, we decided to meet for lunch sometime and exchanged phone numbers.

Mary failed to appear for the first three lunches we scheduled together. Had it been anyone else, I'd have written her off, but I knew that people with mental health issues often have fears and anxiety that lead them to self-destructive behavior. I wanted to be her friend and I had a counterintuitive sense that she wanted the same.

When we finally had lunch on the fourth attempt, I said to her, "Mary, I want to be your friend, but friends are reliable. If we arrange to do something together I expect you to show up and if you can't, I expect you to call and tell me. I'll do the same for you. Okay?"

"Yes," she said. "I'll call in the future."

And she did. For two years she called if she couldn't make it when we had plans. We met every other week, alternating lunch and coffee.

Then I proposed the circus. Soon after we didn't go, we went to lunch together. As we finished eating, I said, "I need to say something about the circus situation. I think you know I was angry that you said you'd go and then changed your mind. What made me angrier is that you lied to me. You gave me two different reasons for not going. I don't care which, if either, reason was true. Honesty is a top priority for me. I'm willing to put this incident behind us but in the future please turn down my offers *before* I've spent money. And lying is unacceptable; I won't have a friend I can't trust. Understood?"

Mary sat quietly through my tirade. She responded to my one-word question with one word, "Yes."

Since the circus debacle, our road has sometimes been rocky, but we have persevered. Currently Mary calls me every three weeks. We make plans and meet, usually for lunch or a movie. It works for both of us. We are friends – in Mary's words, best friends.

What was she thinking
Deanna

> *An honest and profoundly moving essay about facing childhood trauma, combatting addiction, overcoming abuse, changing patterns and building a new life.* ❖ *Your ability to endure and prevail in the face of your litany of hardships and come out not just standing, but standing on top is truly inspiring and sure to offer hope to others going through dark times.* ❖ *Sounds like you have struck pay dirt: sobriety, calm, solid career, and discovering fulfillment in giving back.* ❖ *The author shows great insight into the rocky path to true transformation.*

Leaving two little girls with her abusive husband? Unfortunately, the abuse didn't stop with her. So that's where the story begins.

Foster care sucked, but not as bad as living with my mom and my step dad. Did they have to drink all the time? Would it be too much to ask to have a home of our own, or to stay in one school for more than a year? My sister was the tough one, but was she really? I think she was scared. I know I was.

Another move? In the hills near W. VA no doubt! I was getting ready to graduate high school there, and again, moving? Roger said I could live with him and his family. Wow, what an adventure! I graduated high school, turned 18 that December and was four months pregnant. I never heard from my mom much. She drank a lot and she and my step dad had three more kids, so whatever.

Sure I drank as a teenager, everyone did, but I wasn't raising my kids like that, no way! Not to mention a drunk driver took my sister's life. I hated alcohol. I knew one day God would save me from all this craziness. After 16 years of abuse, He did! I was free, or was I?

Challenge into Change

I met David. This was going to be great! Sure it was for a while, until I broke up with him. When I told him I didn't love him, he squeezed my neck so hard I passed out. Blood was everywhere. Some staples in my head and I was good as new, or was I?

I met Percy. He was so tall and handsome. I thought I had made it this time. We built a nice home, I climbed the corporate ladder where I worked. I was attractive, 34 years old and extremely lonely. He rejected me continuously for 6 years. One night when I complained he didn't show affection, he snapped. Back in the hospital I went!

Now I could afford a nicer place. Leah had left for Colorado for school and my son was married. I just turned 40. I was in great shape, so why did I have to drink? Faced with more heart break and rejection, After 5 years, alcohol took my great job and now it was killing me slowly. The disease crept up on me like a thief in the night. I hated alcohol, didn't I?

Gary was worse than them all. Right out of prison, I was clueless that is was for nearly killing his previous girlfriend. I had broken ribs and stayed in the hospital 6 days with internal injuries. I prayed God would deliver me from all of this and He is faithful, isn't He?

Sober two yrs, managing a medical practice, helping women w/addiction and abuse. After 18 single years, I'm finally marrying a kind, gentle, patient, loving gentleman next month.

God is good? Yes He is!!

I'm Livin' in the Now
Diane Harrell

> *Your optimism and exuberant love of life in the face of your innumerable trials and life-threatening illness is an inspiration and example to us all of how to be in the world. May your bright light shine for many decades to come.* ❖ *A true testament to the power of the human spirit to hold true to the beauty and gifts of the present moment.* ❖ *With this kind of attitude, nothing can stop you.* ❖ *Your story embodies the essence of courage and heart.*

This is my new motto. I have come to a point in my life where I understand that where I am now is the wonderful beginning to continue on this beautiful journey of life. I was just told a couple weeks ago that there are five stages of renal failure and I am in stage four failure. WOW! My first thoughts were, "You are going to die." Then I thought, "We all are going to die one day, and today is not my day."

There was a time when I was ready to throw in the towel. My heart was always heavy because I did not feel I was good enough, smart enough or attractive enough. I was told that by my mother after I became pregnant at 17 – and who else knows you better than your mother, RIGHT? Well, I carried that baggage for years and it really affected my 20's, 30's and 40's, and then in my 50's thoughts of taking my life were looming around my mind. But I was a single mother and I had always wanted to be a good role model to my only child so there was no way I could give up.

I acquired my associate's degree at 55 and still I did not feel that great. I eventually found The Women's Initiative, a wonderful group. I met some of the most beautiful, smart, and good-hearted women from all walks of life and they had had things happen in their lives also. I found myself when I went there. I realized I was looking for love in all the wrong places and blocking my blessings, when true love was always with me all the time.

I am a strong woman of faith now, more than I have ever been, and I know the power of prayer changes things. This journey has been an amazing learning and growth experience. I am grateful for the trials and growing pains. It has brought a tremendous change in my attitude and coping skills and every heartbreak and crying spell has been worth it.

So I say, "Bring it on! That was me then and this is me Now. God's got my back."

Gene
Judith Sullivan

> *Your story is a reminder of what's really important. Not outward appearances and labels, but what is inside a person. Gene challenged your stereotypes and transformed your heart.* ❖ *This touching essay reveals the gifts that others bring into our lives, the yin yang truth that opposites attract . . . and in doing so, learn from one another. In love and in life.* ❖ *This essay describes an openness that is derived from "listening" to the body, to the heart, that helps us get beyond our heads.* ❖ *Simple, powerful, well-crafted mystery, haunting, easy to devour and feeling fulfilled. Thank you.*

The body knows things a long time before the mind catches up to them. I was wondering what my body knew that I didn't.

— Sue Monk Kidd

They had nothing in common. That's what he said on their first date, thanks to Plenty of Fish, an on-line dating service. They were eating at the Aberdeen Barn. Nice for a first date, not the normal coffee andtellyourwholelifehistoryinhalfanhour date. He was right. He was a Republican; she, a Democrat. He was conservative; she liberal. He thought alternative medicine was bogus; that was her profession. He carried a gun and was a member of the NRA. She didn't, and wasn't. He paid for dinner.

On the second date they ate on the downtown mall and then went for a walk. He held her hand and put it with his, in his pocket. She was suspicious at first, but then found it oddly comforting. On the third date he tried to kiss her and at the last minute she turned her head and he kissed her ear. She was surprised at that. She hadn't planned on turning her head. He asked if she wanted to go out again and she said yes. That surprised her too.

A few months later he said that if she had said no, he would have sent her flowers and chocolate. She thought that maybe she should have said no. She loved chocolate and flowers.

He died about two years later. In the meantime she found out that she was in love with him. There was a feeling of comfort and safety with him she had never had before. She didn't even get upset about the guns. They found out that at their core they had a lot in common. Around the edges they were very different. But they continued to respect each other. He loved to drive and she didn't. But when she was with him in the car, she noticed that she was more relaxed than she had ever been before. At night he would say sweet things to her that while her head was saying it probably was a line, her body was shaken to its core. No one had ever said those things to her before. When he held her, she felt like she was home. They could sit together doing separate projects and feel connected and happy.

Her head would never have fallen in love with him. He didn't fit her image. But he did have such twinkly eyes. Something else seemed to be happening. Her body kept telling her in different small ways that this man counted. This man was important. This man really loved her. Not because of her job or credentials, but just because she was loveable.

After he died everyone said how lucky he was to have had her in his life. She thought how lucky she was to have had him in her life, even for a short while. It changed how she looked at everything.

Prescription: Yoga
Kellie L. Silcio

> *A powerful story about reconnecting with one's essence through movement, breath and a profound understanding that all is impermanent. Keep practicing. Keep listening to the essence of your soul.* ❖ *Your essay is an inspiring, compelling call to action to those suffering from depression to give yoga a try. How joyful that you found yourself "underneath the dark layers that covered" you for so long.* ❖ *Your love of yoga rings clear through your marvelous descriptive prose.* ❖ *How inspiring you sought and found!*

I have a long history of depression, which was greatly exacerbated when I moved from New Orleans to Charlottesville in 2009. I knew no one and quickly left the graduate program that brought me here. I had developed a very strict plan for my future after Hurricane Katrina. It gave me focus and stability during a very confusing time; then I moved halfway across the country to have it fall apart. I became isolated in my apartment. I was uncomfortable in any social situation – even browsing store aisles. I hated myself. I hated this town. I stopped taking care of myself and gained 25 pounds.

Skip forward to 2012 – my worst year in Virginia. My life and sense of purpose continued to decline. I felt so desperate that I overdosed on a medication. During recovery, I spent two weeks at a wellness center where I was introduced to meditation, acupuncture, and yoga. I want to add these elements to my life, but they were hard to hold onto on my own.

I struggled until January of this year when I attended my first yoga class. Not only was I shocked that I brought myself to a new experience, I felt an intense awakening within my body. As I stretched, my weakened body and spirit seemed to radiate two words to my mind: THANK YOU. I couldn't believe how quickly my energy, strength and flexibility increased. The yoga studio was the first place I felt comfortable going to by myself. As I continued to engage, this opening began translating to my whole life.

After two years of feeling incompetent, I WANT to find employment. I WANT to contribute to this society which I no longer hate. I currently volunteer with two local organizations. My yoga study continues with a level of dedication I have not observed within myself for years! And I smile. Every day. Yoga is THE BEST antidepressant I've found – and I've tried many. I inspire myself and others. I've lost count of how many Facebook friends have decided to try yoga after seeing updates on my physical, mental, and spiritual growth. I'm making several local friends. I now have a deep sense of purpose, though I've lost the need for control over every aspect of my future. I've learned to set honest intentions. I trust myself and my world.

For the first time in my memory, I can tell you that I am NOT depressed. I have bad days, but I know tomorrow will be brighter and nothing is permanent. I am only "stuck" in life if I choose to be. I want to live, and I want to give. I practice yoga daily with the intention of becoming a teacher. My purpose in life is to facilitate healing for others, and I'm excited to discover in which ways I will be able to do so. More than anything, I've found a sense of calm and comfort within myself that was unknown to me.

I can't tell you how I know this will last. I can just say that I have found myself – not a new self. The person I've always been – underneath the dark layers that covered me for so long. I remember the traumas of my past; they just no longer rule me. They never will again. Without yoga, I would still be lost. But now I know love, friendship, and I know the power I have within me. No one can or will ever take that away.

How did you get here. An Odyssey
Linda

> *Your odyssey from "bruised and needy" and "petrified-stuck" to the self-supporting and self-respecting woman you are today is truly inspirational ❖ An inspiring essay about bravery, courage, accepting support and finding self-sufficiency. ❖ A wonderful essay about great perseverance and of how others in our lives can step in and help at just the right moment. ❖ A long road from Kansas to Charlottesville, paved with many obstacles and broken pathways, plus goodwill of family and friends. An odyssey for sure! Your strength and determination suit you well — culminating in wholeness and redemption.*

-What, how did I end up in Charlottesville?

The simple answer is that I needed a job.

-What is the complicated answer?

I don't usually talk about that, but I was a newly single parent, feeling quite bruised and needy. The jobs that I wanted in Lawrence, KS, were held by folks who were not going to be leaving anytime soon, so I had to start looking further afield. I had been unemployed 6 months and needed to get my life together. All my relatives lived in New Jersey and I wanted to be close enough to bring the kids to visit them. So I started looking in college towns east of Lawrence. There aren't many you know.

So I packed the car, our beloved old VW bug and left. A dear neighbor treated us to a parting breakfast at McDonald's and gave the kids $10 each for souvenirs as we traveled. We got to Durham the second day, which I considered briefly, but realized at that time that I wouldn't be able to apply for jobs and take care of the kids, clearly I had not done enough planning. I asked for help, not something I did often. I made a desperate call to my mother and found she had just been laid off from her job. I put the kids on a plane and they stayed with her for the next five weeks, a bonding experience for them all. Then I started the car and drove straight through to Virginia Beach, afraid to turn it off for fear it would never start again. At this point I was petrified-stuck without my kids and without my vehicle.

-That was an awfully brave thing to do.

I stayed in Virginia Beach for 4 weeks, with the parents of friends, an offer that came out of another desperate plea for help. I found a temp job in a doctor's office and used the buses. The VW was a bigger problem and one that I did not have the means to solve. I made a call to my ex and groveled, without success. I finally called a friend back in Lawrence, who forwarded me enough money to repair my vehicle. Years later, when I began to repay his generosity he tore up the check and suggested that at some point when I was able I pay it forward., which I am still doing in little ways as I can.

I got a job on my first application in Charlottesville, used the McDonald's telephone across the street as my contact number and made up an address for the application, then updated it once I saved enough that I could leave the Salvation Army into an apartment – no beds, but pots pans a key and my family altogether, with the help of a lot of people along the way. A path to self-support and self-respect.

Challenge into Change

Polio: A Lifetime Challenge
Wilma T. Mangione

> *A true testament to the power of an individual to see challenges as opportunities. I hope that the author will dive into her pursuit of writing and artistic endeavors with the same tenacity she has shown throughout her inspiring life.* ❖ *Your optimism and gratitude for life shine through in this story of childhood illness that has shadowed you for a lifetime. Your ability to embrace life and always see the glass half full is inspiration to us all.* ❖ *The writer creates a vivid description of what it is like to live with a frightening disease, while demonstrating strength and adaptability in recovery.* ❖ *A brilliantly brave life story, shared in ten paragraphs. Very well crafted. Your willingness and open heart to see opportunity in your profound challenges is indeed captivating and inspiring.*

"With every challenge, comes an opportunity," my mother said, trying to talk me into being more agreeable about doing my exercises. Adding a new role to her usual household duties, she was now my physical therapist, three times a day.

I had just returned home from a three-month stay in a children's hospital where I was treated for acute poliomyelitis, a crippling, killing disease and a national epidemic. This was 1944 and no vaccine was yet available to control the spread of this paralyzing virus. I was barely eleven years old when I became ill and was immediately rushed by ambulance to the nearest facility receiving polio patients, 75 miles away. My right arm was paralyzed.

Now, three months later, my hand was getting stronger but the muscles used to lift my arm were not. My right leg was weak but I was able to walk

I had been through "The Sister Kenny Treatment." Steam-heated "hot packs" were wrapped around the torso and limbs repeatedly, throughout the day. I also had massage and exercise to stretch and soothe my cramping muscles.

For the first three weeks of my hospital stay, I was in isolation. No Visitors! This was heart breaking for me and my mother. She stayed nearby, but could neither see nor talk to me. I kept looking out my window, hoping she would be there to wave at me. But that was not allowed.

My family was also in isolation—at home. A quarantine sign stayed on the door for two weeks. My father stayed home from work. My sister and two brothers stayed home from school. Groceries were delivered but were left on the porch.

When I returned home, I started back to school but this proved too tiring. My doctor decided that I should wait until fall to return. Resting and a summer of play made me stronger and ready to try again in September. Understanding teachers helped me to adjust to my new classes.

Although I did not regain full use of my arm, I have led a normal life. I was happy in school, and able to participate in most of the activities. After college, I married, had two wonderful children, and have two grandchildren. I had a career in two fields that I love, Environmental Planning and Historic Preservation. I have been able to maintain my physical health throughout my life by riding horseback, teaching riding lessons and yoga.

Like many aging polio survivors, I am faced with the threat of Post Polio Syndrome (PPPS). Because the polio virus depletes and weakens the neurons of muscles, the overworked and compensating muscles and joints are susceptible to greater wear and tear. Eventually, this can lead to PPS and a more limited mobility.

Thus new challenge gives me the opportunity to enjoy being a spectator and pursue my writing and artistic interests.

ABOUT THE WOMEN'S INITIATIVE

The Women's Initiative was founded in 2007 in Charlottesville, Virginia, in response to a profound community need for affordable mental health services for women. From its inception, the mission has been to provide effective individual counseling services, social support groups and education to empower women to transform challenging life situations into opportunities for renewed wellbeing and personal growth. The conviction that all women should have access to vital mental health services, regardless of their ability to pay, animates the daily work of The Women's Initiative.

Our individual counseling services and facilitated support groups empower women to gain freedom from mental illnesses that are diminishing their lives. Our strong, diverse team of therapists bring more than 150 years of combined counseling experience in a variety of specialties. Comprehensive assessments and individualized treatment plans are designed to address each woman's unique personal history and distinct needs.

Please visit us at www.thewomensinitiative.org.

the women's initiative

empowering women in times of challenge & change

ABOUT THE JUDGES
ಸಾಧ

KERRY DAY
Compassion, intuition, nurturing presence, wisdom and laughter are just a few adjectives that describe Kerry Day, the first Executive Director of The Women's Initiative from 2008 to 2011. A dedicated Ashtanga yoga practitioner and teacher, Kerry is the author of *Life in the Front Yard* and the mother of three fabulous children. One day Kerry and her husband hope to travel the world.

PIE DUMAS
Pie Dumas of Scottsville, VA, is an author and Certified Life Coach. She is currently writing an inspirational resource book, featuring stories from men and women behind bars, recounting their experience with life-changing prison programs. In 2005, she published her memoir, *Pieces of Pie: Surviving Love*, a story of transformation and healing.

LESLEY FOSTER
A former communications professional from Washington, DC, and Portland, OR, Lesley Foster is an experienced feature writer, copywriter, magazine editor, and writing and speech consultant. As owner of Ink & Inquiry, she leads contemplative writing workshops exploring innovative ways to use writing as a tool for personal growth, creative problem-solving, and engaging higher capacities. Since 2010, Lesley has led numerous writing workshops at The Women's Initiative and was contest coordinator for this year's Challenge into Change Essay Contest.

DR. MARGARET PLEWS-OGAN
Dr. Plews-Ogan is associate professor of medicine and chief of the Division of General Medicine, Geriatrics, and Palliative Medicine at the University of Virginia. She is also lead investigator and director of the UVA center for Appreciative Practice, a positive culture transformation initiative. Dr. Plews-Ogan's is also a co-author

(along with Justine Owens, PhD and Natalie May, PhD) of *Choosing Wisdom: Strategies and Inspiration for Growing Through Life-Changing Difficulties*. This inspirational book was featured at the 2013 Virginia Festival of the Book including a panel discussion sponsored by The Women's Initiative.

LIZ DORN (Contest Director and Tie-breaker Judge)
The Women's Initiative hired Liz Dorn as its first Development Director in Spring 2011. A writer by trade, Liz offsets writing-for-work and other fundraising duties with dabbling into nonfiction and poetry. Her first collaborative work where she served as concept editor, "Paths Are Made By Walking," was published in 2003 by Time Warner.